Shinrigaku

Basic Ninja Mind Disciplines

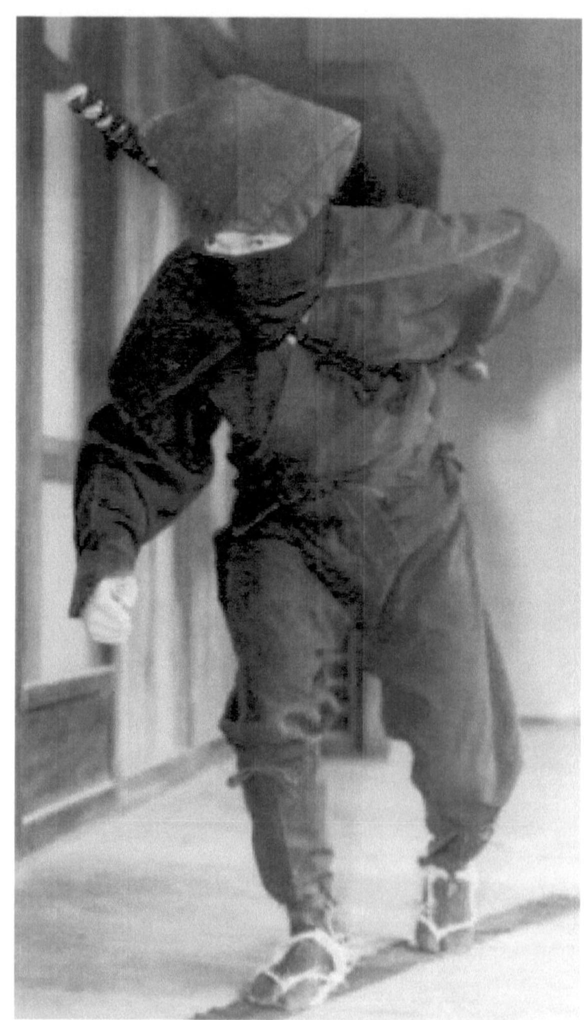

Mugei-mumei, No Art, No Name
The First Law of Ninjutsu

SHINRIGAKU

Basic Ninja Mind Disciplines

JAMES LORIEGA

LOST ARTS
PUBLICATIONS

SHINRIGAKU Basic Ninja Mind Disciplines

First Printing:November 2021

ISBN: 978-1-7947-5750-9

Lost Arts Publications
Brooklyn, NY 11235

LOST ARTS
PUBLICATIONS

Dedication

To Naomi,
who has mastered these skills
without ever setting foot in a Dojo.

O divine art of subtlety and secrecy!
Through you we learn to be invisible,
through you, we are inaudible; and hence
we can hold the enemy's fate in our hands...

—Sonbu
Sonshi, Book VI

Disclaimer Notice

The information presented in this book is not intended to be interpreted as legal advice; nor is the description of the techniques meant to take the place of proper instruction under the tutelage and supervision of a qualified and competent instructor. The techniques contained herein reflect the injurious methods used in extreme life-or-death situations. As such, they are dangerous, if not lethal, to use. They are presented here solely for informational purposes, and neither the author nor the publisher is responsible for their use.

SHINRIGAKU

Basic Ninja Mind Disciplines

CONTENTS

PREFACE

This book, part of the Shinobi-no-Michi series, is an abridged version of A Legacy of Lost Arts. It is designed to serve as a quick reference on the basic mental skills of the shinobi, but excludes the historical context found in Legacy. In its current form, it can be used as a checklist for the development and continued maintenance of the disciplines described, which are a defining component of ninjutsu. If these mind disciplines are ignored, the physical training in ninjutsu can become almost indistinguishable from the quotidian block-punch-and-throw combat arts. This in fact is already the case in those dojo that purport to teach ninjutsu.

Jujutsu in a Black Uniform

When my students attend an outside "ninjutsu" seminar, or when I visit another "ninjutsu" instructor's dojo, what we invariably find being taught is *Jujutsu in a Black Gi,* as we privately refer to it. (Remember that traditionally jujutsu *also* included the use of weapons.) These seminars and dojo have an exclusive focus on self defense techniques and combat sparring, and sometimes a limited emphasis on the use of weapons. But that is generally the extent of their "ninjutsu."

Of course, self-defense techniques and combat abilities are necessary skills, as is the ability to use traditional Japanese weapons—but ninjutsu is the art of Espionage! Where is the *intelligence gathering*? The *surreptitious entry and exit methods*? The *covert strategies*? The *counters to the enemy's strategies*? The *invisible accomplishment* of one's objectives?

This is *not* ninjutsu

In short, what do these "ninjutsu" dojo and seminars offer to set themselves apart from the ubiquitous jujutsu or self-defense[1] schools that teach the same or similar skills? Is it their black jujutsu uniforms or fancy "ninja" patches that make what they teach "ninjutsu?" While unarmed and armed fighting arts are a part of ninjutsu, the art relies on many more arts that are not being taught in dojo around the world. It is those arts that we will begin to introduce in this book.

INTRODUCTION

Ninjutsu's origins are understandably not as well-documented as those of other mainstream Japanese martial arts because, as we know today, the art's genesis and evolution was of needs cloaked in secrecy. Yet those origins are *not* necessarily lost in "the vague and murky mists of time," and though details may be missing or unknown, ninjutsu's evolution is *knowable*. And it begins in China.

The Art of War

The Art of War (or, ***Bing Fa***) is a Chinese military treatise that dates back to the 5th century BC. Attributed to the warrior philosopher ***Sun Tzu***, *The Art of War* is comprised of thirteen chapters, each of which addresses a specific aspect of warfare. As such, the treatise is commonly regarded as a definitive work on military strategy and tactics and has long been the most influential strategy text in East Asia.

By Unconventional Means

Sun Tzu's perception of war was not so much a matter of destroying the enemy materially and physically (though that was always an option), but of unsettling the enemy psychologically. Operationally, he lays great stress on the employment of secret agents, as well as on ***kueitao***, which translates as *deception* or *unconventional means*. Thus Sunzi commends operations that will harm enemy morale—*splitting alliances, evading battle, attacking by surprise*.

The Art of War was introduced to Japan around750 AD. The treatise quickly became popular among Japanese generals, and historical records indicate that Japanese warriors were applying the precepts of *The Art of War* as early as 760 AD. A key component of military victory is the collecting of information to inform decisions. As relates to the art of ninjutsu, Sun Tzu devotes the final chapter of The Art of War to espionage.

The Mind As A Weapon

As history has demonstrated, ninjutsu is an art first practiced in the mind—and it is a person's mindset that makes them a ninja. As ninjutsu practitioners, we are more fortunate than martial artists because the art we practice encompasses a vast number of philosophical, psychological, and physical teachings that serve to guide our thinking and inform our *actions.* To claim to be actually practicing this art, we must train in more disciplines than simply fighting. Many more.

The Mind as Weapon

The ninja was not paid to engage the enemy but to *outsmart* him. While the samurai was paid to fight, the ninja was paid to do what the samurai could not. The ninja's profession mandated that he use his mental weapons before he resorted to physical ones.

Although in modern Japanese usage the term *shinrigaku* is used to mean "psychology," it was originally used as blanket term for the variety of *mental strategies* used by the ninja against an enemy or opponent. The term encompassed covert methods of character assessment, face-reading, hypnotism, persuasion, elicitation (a form of covert interrogation), manipulation, and related skills.

In **The Secret Thoughts and Strategies of the Ninja**, Heishichiro Okuse observes that ninja regarded nothing as impossible[1] and scientifically applied what he calls "brain power" to every problem they encountered. He further identified the non-physical aspects of ninjutsu as being the key to a successful career as a shinobi.

In **Ninja, The Invisible Assassins**, Adams notes,

> [The ninja] *had to have their wits about them at all times and* [to] *work out complicated problems on the spot. They learned to sharpen their perception and insight, developing their instincts to a point that seemed almost superhuman.*

That methodical *"sharpening of perception and insight",* and *"development of instincts to a point that seemed almost superhu*man" is what is known in ninjutsu as *shinrigaku.* Regrettably, it is taught in merely a handful of modern ninjutsu dojo.

Mind Disciplines

Mind disciplines evolved over time in feudal Japan, when the potential for life-or-death engagements was present at all times. The disciplines warned the *bushi* and *shinobi* if danger was imminent, allowing them to preempt the threat. More importantly, by the early insight they provided, these disciplines enabled feudal warriors to avert unnecessary fighting.

Shinrigaku served the *shinobi* in the same manner but for a different reason. The *shinobi* had to avoid open combat for purposes of

1 In the third film of the 1960s *Shinobi-no-Mono* series, Ishikawa Goemon tells Hattori Hanzo, "*The greatest shame for a shinobi is to assume any objective is impossible.*"

anonymity and the integrity of their assignments. Unless they planned to leave a trail of dead or injured bodies that would lead to their being discovered, the *shinobi* also relied on disciplines that alerted them to potential danger and precluded the need for combat or killing.

"The greatest shame for a shinobi... is to assume that any objective is impossible."
—Ishikawa Goemon to Hattori Hanzo

Traditionally, these disciplines were acquired by the historical *bushi* and *shinobi* in the practice of their *koryū bugei* arts. Today, they have been virtually lost in the wake of the *gendai budo*. This is because once the possibility of someone lying in wait with sharp *katana* is no longer a likely threat and the skills that once evolved for averting such once-prevalent threats have waned or died. The chapters that immediately follow will each address discrete components of *shinrigaku*.

The tenets that follow have been taught in ninjutsu for centuries. I chose them from among countless others as examples of how ninjutsu's teachings are perennial and relevant to the current pandemic situation. By keeping the tenets in mind we can use them to re-frame our present perspective.

MUGEI-MUMEI

MUGEI-MUMEI is said to be the first law of ninjutsu. It dictates that the ninja must never be seen as a ninja; must never be seen as a spy; must never be seen as a threat; and must never do anything that draws attention to himself. Yet, how many practitioners today are willing to abide by that tenet—and to forfeit their fifteen minutes of fame?

Many ninjutsu practitioners, instructors as well as students, should consider removing their decoratively-colored patches, take off the red *hakama* with matching *tabi*, relinquish the self-awarded titles they smugly lay claim to, and give some thought to becoming more anonymous and less identifiable. If we seek to sincerely emulate the historical *shinobi*, then our goal must be to become unnoticeable.

The Lost and Forgotten Ways

A principal purpose of this book is to remind—in some cases, *inform*—shinobi enthusiasts that taijutsu is *not* ninjutsu, and to provide a brief but detailed overview of some traditional ninjutsu practices, lending perspective to some of the lesser-known aspects of the art. Although instruction in the combat arts is widely available, there is a disproportionate scarcity of resources related to ninjutsu's mental and psychological strategies and tactics. Information (to say nothing of instruction) on such areas as *assessing an enemy, reading his character, understanding his proclivities*, and *influencing his actions,* to name but a few skills, have been virtually neglected by the "experts."

This book hopes to clarify that ninjutsu is first and foremost the *Art of Protection Against Danger*, as the late martial scholar, Donn F. Draeger, defined it. As per that eloquent definition, ninjutsu fully embodies the original philosophies and priorities set down by Sonbu in his *Sonshi-no-Heiho* twenty-five centuries ago.

In that treatise, (the thirteenth chapter of which became the inspiration for ninjutsu), Sonbu speaks in detail about *intelligence-gathering*, *espionage*, *subterfuge*, *deception* and other related strategic aspects that are inherent to the ninja's art. Sonbu's mandate for *knowing your enemy*, so over-used today, was the *raison d'etre* for the practice of ninjutsu:

> *What enables the wise sovereign and the good general to strike and conquer, and achieve things beyond the reach of ordinary men, is **foreknowledge**.*

Nowhere in the seventeen different translations of **The Art of War** in my library does Sonbu ever exhort the importance of *taijutsu, jujutsu*, or wearing varicolored belts. If that has been your focus up till now, it's time to step off the mat and read a book on ninjutsu—*any book*: Draeger's **The Art of Invisibility**. Adams' **The Invisible Assassins**. Hayes's **The Ninja and Their Secret Fighting Art**. It's also time to realize that the historical ninja's professional objective was *anonymity*, not self-aggrandizement; and that your skill in ninjutsu is *not* measured by how well you fight, but by how well you accomplish your goals *without having to*!

METSUKE

If your mind is preoccupied with one leaf, you don't see the others; if you don't set your attention on one, you will see hundreds and thousands of leaves.

—Yagyu Munenori
The Way of the Living Sword

METSUKE, like most Japanese words, carries multiple meanings in the *koryū* arts. Literally "ability to see," *metsuke* can be used to describe—1) the way in which you *gaze* at an opponent; 2) the way in which you *view* a dangerous situation; or 3) the manner in which you *regard* a threatening environment. You use your eyes perceptively, but *without* obsessive focus or undue analysis. Within the context of ninjutsu and the *koryū bugei*, metsuke can be expressed as a *piercing* or *penetrating gaze,* and is an attribute developed through training and experience.

Your Facial Expression

It is first important to realize that facial expressions and demeanor openly provide information about an individual's state of mind. Knowing that, you must strive to keep your own face *impassive* in combat so that it cannot be easily read by an astute enemy.

You must also avoid attempts to intimidate with your expression, for a person who makes exaggerated, fearsome, or even threatening faces is often perceived to be insecure or desperate, like a child trying to intimidate an adult. You can actively assess and analyze your enemy, but your discoveries and decisions must not be reflected on you face.

Mokushin and Ganriki

In the information the follows, we will refer to the metsuke as the *combat gaze*. Although there are many ways to apply the combat gaze, there are two principal ways that relate directly to active combative engagement. The first way is called *mokushin, or* "the eye of the mind;" the second way is *ganriki,* or "the power of the eye."

Mokushin

Mokushin involves seeing with the *mind's eye,* often to enclose and envelope an opponent. This is best accomplished by maintaining a *calm, natural,* and *confident* expression on the face. Projecting a serene demeanor regardless of what happens is much more unsettling to an enemy than an angry war face. A calm face allows you to remain calm, and this in turn helps you to observe and assess the enemy—without wasting energy by attempting to intimidate or deceive him.

Ganriki

When your are fully intent on defeating your enemy, your calm face will naturally take on a piercing and intense quality called *ganriki.* Ganriki is a *sharp, penetrating gaze* that sees an enemy's intentions and can be used to dominate and control him. Just as importantly, your enemy will understand this look, as well.

It can be challenging to depict these two types of metsuke in photos because they occur naturally in combat and cannot be modeled or "posed." To clarify, the two photographs of Toshiro Mifune on the next page, *acted* as they are, may help differentiate *mokushin* from *genriki.*

***Mokushin* (below) is the calm, confident, and observant gaze.**

Mokushin

***Ganriki* (above) is the sharp, piercing, and penetrating gaze.**

Some traditions teach that one should look directly at the opponent's eyes. Other traditions warn that looking at the eyes can be mesmerizing, and that one should instead look at the whole person from head to toe. Holding your combat gaze just above the bridge of the enemy's nose, between his two eyebrows, is a practical compromise. From there you can also sense intentions from his subtle changes and shifts in posture.

In **The Book of Five Rings** legendary master swordsman, Musashi Miyamoto, eloquently provides the following advice with respect to the combat gaze (although Musashi's many translators do not know enough to call it that):

> *View situations in a sweeping, broad fashion.*
> *The two ways of seeing things are* **kan** (observing) *and* **ken** (looking). *Kan, observing, is strong; ken, looking, weak. Seeing distant things as if they are close at hand and seeing close things as if they are distant is unique to the art of combat.*

Pay Attention *Without* Looking

Both unfocused and focused seeing form the spectrum of the combat gaze; but metsuke is not merely unfocused or focused seeing. It requires *paying attention*. Never look into the opponent's eyes because this distracts your clarity of mind. Before he founded **aikido**, *Ueshiba Morihei*, who had trained rigorously in *Daito-ryu* and other *koryū* arts, wrote:

> *Do not look at the opponent's eyes, or your mind will be drawn into them. Do not look at his sword, or you will be slain by it. Do not look at him, or your spirit will be distracted. True budo is the cultivation of attraction with which to draw the*

whole opponent to you. All I have to do is keep standing this way.

Thus *mokushin* is used to gaze beyond the enemy, taking in the whole person, noticing every aspect, and thus reading any intention or movement immediately. *Ganriki* is used to control the enemy because it enables you to control the distance between you (*ma-ai)*, and thus allows you to appropriately intercept.

Enzan-no-Metsuke

The phrase *enzan-no-metsuke* translates as, "Gazing at a distant mountain," and represents a common practice used for developing metsuke. It involves focusing the eyes at a distance, which is crucial to developing the mental vision necessary in combat, instead of looking at what is directly in front of you.

To begin *enzan-no-metsuke*, relax your vision and look as if gazing at the panorama behind the training partner. You will begin seeing your surroundings in proper perspective, without locking your focus on a particular detail—which can prevent you from seeing everything else. *See photo on next page.*

What You Don't Use ...

Disregard for using the combat gaze not only robs you of its advantages in a personal combat engagement, but can also atrophy of these faculties. In our “civilized” world we are taught only to look, and thereby we become blind. Believing that it is enough to *see*, we cease to *notice*.

***Enzan-no-Metsuke*, Gazing at a Distant Mountain**

For the *bushi* and *shinobi*, there were ways to look through water, and there were ways to see into fire. Today, there is more to see in our air than city people would want to know exists! Everything on the planet contains dimensions not readily perceivable to the untrained eye. To seen them, train your eyes!

BANPEN FUGYO

Ten Thousand Changes; No Surprises

BANPEN FUGYO translates literally as "Ten Thousand Changes; No Surprises." This tenet reminds us to never be surprised by change, no matter how unexpected. While this is admittedly a challenging attribute to develop, novices can begin by never respond to being surprised by reacting in a visibly surprised manner. Do not allow yourself to become the "deer in the headlights."

A shinobi maintains his mental equilibrium regardless of how off-balance he may actually feel. He never allows whatever has caught him off guard to alter is outward demeanor; thus, he may experience *ten thousand changes* but will outwardly demonstrate *no surprise.*

Banpen fugyo will serve you in keeping your wits about you during what may feel like uncertain times; *uncertain times such as these*. You must maintain a positive perspective, remembering that nothing good comes from panicking. Turn your legitimate concern into a catalyst for exercising extreme care in all you do. Engage in constructive "What if" thinking and help those around you to do likewise.

Fudoshin

Practice to adopt an attitude of **fudoshin**. The term fudoshin is comprised of *fudo*, or "immovable," and *shin*, which mean "heart," or "mind," or both. Possessing an attitude of fudoshin means you cannot be made to feel ruffled or frazzled. Having fudoshin means that, regardless of what distress you may feel, you remain in control and unperturbed.

Fudoshin—in control and unperturbed

Possessing fudoshin facilitates banpen fugyo, and banpen fugyo enhances fudoshin. You may know fear, but you will never panic! And you may experience a thousand changes, but within you *they will evoke no change.*

Haragei

If you know the enemy and know yourself, you need not fear the result of a hundred battles. If you know yourself but not the enemy, for every victory gained you will also suffer a defeat. If you know neither the enemy nor yourself, you will succumb in every battle.

—Sonbu
Sonshi, Book III

The above quote may sound trite today, but during Japan's bloody *Warring States Era* (1467—1601) it was considered sage military advice. The advice is actually twofold: 1) to *know your enemy*, and 2) to *know yourself*. You begin with the obvious and familiar, *knowing yourself*; or more precisely, *developing* yourself. The core attribute on which most, if not all, of the ninja's abilities rely is *haragei*.

Haragei enables the *shinobi* to sense threats and read intentions

The following anecdote concerning *Yagyu Munenori*, who was the personal sword instructor to Shogun Iemitsu, is an excellent example of haragei. Writer Makoto Sugawara recounts it as follows:

> *When Munenori was granted an audience with the shogun, Iemitsu, he sat down, put his hands on the tatami floor, as retainers always did to show their respect to their master.*
>
> *Suddenly, Iemitsu thrust a spear at the "unsuspecting" Munenori—and was surprised to find himself lying flat on his back!*
>
> *Munenori had sensed the shogun's intention before a move had been made, and swept Iemitsu's legs out from under him at the instant of the thrust.*

What alerted Munenori to the shogun's failed surprise attack was his keenly-developed sense of *haragei*.

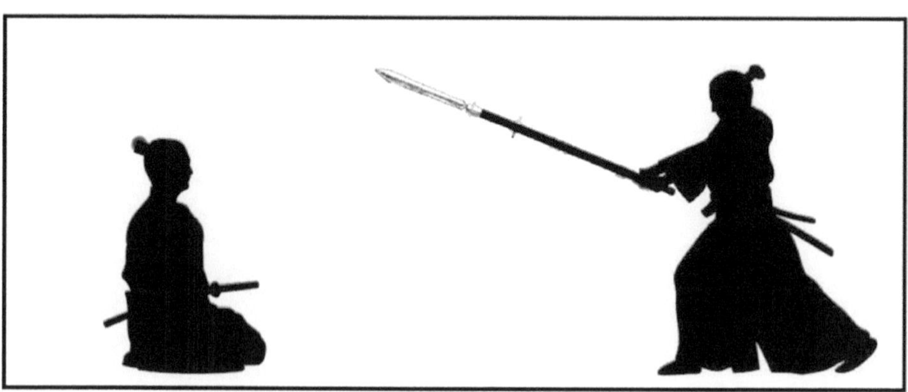

Haragei

In the *koryū bugei*, haragei refers to a sense or quality that enables the *bushi* and *shinobi* to anticipate danger or perceive an opponent's intentions. Additionally, in a non-combative context haragei can refer to a highly-tuned intuition that allows a person to grasp the true nature of a situation independently of verbal communication or deductive reasoning. A person with haragei will be able to see behind what another person says to what they really mean—and will also be able to successfully hide his own true intentions, if and when necessary.

It is easy to see how this applies to *koryū* arts, since the process of a conflict usually involves *hiding your own true intent while discovering the intentions of the enemy* and using that information to devise various stratagems to defeat him. This, in fact, is how the ninja traditionally operated—but it can only be accomplished when one has developed the haragei needed to see through an enemy's stratagems. On the physical level, this is accomplished by learning to remain *calm* and *unruffled*[2], thus allowing the enemy's intent to become clear.

The term haragei is derived from the words *hara*, or "stomach," and *gei*, which is an "art" or "craft." We have all experienced the feeling that we *know* information about an individual or situations in advance, which we may regard as a *hunch* or a *gut feeling*. We do not arrive at such conclusions by means of logic or detailed analysis; instead, these insights often come as a flash of information or a sense of impending danger. It is this heightened form of intuition that the samurai and ninja knew it as haragei.

2 Expressed as *hara ga suwatte iru*

Developing Your Haragei

In our fast-paced world there is simply not enough time to digest all the information that is available. Decisions have to be made quickly. Research tells us that 50% of decisions made logically are later proven to be wrong. This is why people taking written exams are often advised to adhere to their first (gut) responses or answers and disregard any subsequent impulse to second-guess or change them.

Discover your enemy's intentions while concealing your own

Haragei can be developed and accessed intentionally, but only if you train and nurture it. There are many formal methods used for this, as well as some informal modern methods. The best-known method is used in many *koryū* arts and involves a detailed process that can be practiced at home or in the dojo.

Kiaijutsu

With time you will be able to beat swordsmen with your hands, and to defeat people by using your eyes ... And because strategy develops the mind, with sufficient training you will be able to vanquish people with your spirit. When you have reached this point, will it not mean that you are invincible?

—Musashi Miyamoto

The Book of Five Rings

KIAIJUTSU is another one of the many *shinrigaku* disciplines that began to fade away with the decline of the *koryū bugei.* Though *gendai budo* practitioners believe they practice *kiaijutsu*, few of them understand the concept in its entirety. Much of the confusion regarding the subject derives from the fact that those attempting to define kiaijutsu do so from the insular perspective of the individual arts they practice.

Chief among them are the practitioners of judo and karate who, somewhat predictably, approach the subject from near-polar extremes. Add to this the fact that the arts mentioned above are *not koryū bugei* —from which the disciplines of kiai evolved—and one can see how the explanations posited by modern practitioners are, at best, one-sided and, at worst, speculative. Though I am not a practitioner of the *gendai budo*, my statements are based on what some past notable exponents have written and opined with regard to the nature of kiai.

Focused Intent

Kiaijutsu is actually the art of *focusing and directing intent*. The kiai—which can be loud or silent, and anything in between—is the manifestation of that focused intent. Moreover the kiai, and kiaijutsu in general, is not always *martial* in application or effect. The concept of kiaijutsu can be compared to a very sharp knife, which can be used for a variety of purposes: in the hands of a warrior it can be used to *hurt* while in the hands of a surgeon it can be used to *heal*. The sole determinant of the outcome is, yes, the wielder's *intent*.

The Blade of the Mind

Having always been intrigued by the concept of the kiai, I began researching the rudiments of its use. I understood that kiaijutsu is the harnessing and focusing of intent but had no idea as to the various forms of kiai that existed. Discovering those forms led to learning the different ways in which the kiai could be delivered and applied.

There are three fundamental stages of skill in kiaijutsu:

- In the *first* stage, kiaijutsu is applied through your **actions**. The studied use of certain actions can communicate your intent and accomplish your desired outcome.
- In the *second* stage, kiaijutsu is applied by means of **words** and sounds. This is the stage of kiaijutsu that most martial artists are familiar with—the screaming and yelling you hear in many karate schools.
- In the *third* stage—for now, a theoretical one—kiaijutsu is applied through the use of **thoughts**. If you can imagine accomplishing the same results you're already familiar with by merely thinking, *that* would resemble kiaijutsu at the third

stage. That rare third stage of kiaijutsu can be referred to as "the *blade of the mind*."

Musashi Miyamoto's Kiaijutsu

Though one might easily disregard the *blade of the mind* theory as mere speculation, let us return briefly to Musashi's quote at that the start of this chapter and dissect it in context of the three stages.

"... With time you will be able to beat swordsmen with your hands," is an example of a physical **action** of the *body*, enhanced by the kiai.

"... *and to defeat people by using your eyes*." Although no **words** are spoken in Musashi's observation, the defeat is manifested non-vocally by means of what is *communicated by the eyes.*

"... And because strategy develops the mind, with sufficient training you will be able to vanquish people with your spirit." Here, the terms *mind* and *spirit* can be easily equated with one's **will**. Thus, Musashi's entire quote is in fact an explanation of how the kiai naturally develops and is utilized through the body, the word, or the mind.

Musashi ends this particular quote by saying, "*When you have reached this point, will it not mean that you are invincible?*" This can be interpreted as a summary of what the fully-developed ability in kiaijutsu ultimately provides.

Projecting the Intent to Kill

In accepting that kiai is the deliberate harnessing and projection of an individual's intent, we can understand how, when that intent is so focused that it permeates through the individual's entire being, it can be *tangible* and felt by those around him.

It is believed that when intending to kill, all living things project their intention in a distinct manner. In the animal kingdom, there can be no more impressive a manifestation of this phenomenon than the lion's roar which, with enough force to send dust clouds into the air, rattle trees, and travel upwards to great distances, can easily shock prey at close-range into temporary paralysis. This results in what ninjutsu practitioners refer to as the *sakki* (殺気), the so-called *force of the killer*. Once an individual has harnessed his energies and focused his whole being toward an intention—in this case, to kill—others are likely to feel it projected outward through the non-vocal *kiai*.

While this may sound utterly fantastic, we are not speaking of trying to break bricks and boards, or the other recent or silly uses of *kiai*. The art was never intended for that. What we are speaking of is stopping a potential attacker in hs tracks *without* taking a stance, or raising a fist, *or* even uttering a kiai. That is the epitome of *channeling intent*. I saw one of my *shinrigaku* instructors do it, as well. It takes time and commitment to develop, like other elements of the physical martial arts, but it is indisputably an achievable skill.

As many readers already realize, there are manifestations of *kiai* in areas that are unrelated to the martial arts[3]. For example—

- An extremely perturbed or angry individual, who at the same time chooses to exercise self-restraint, will threateningly **glare** at the person "causing" his anger. This threatening glare—sometimes called *dagger eyes*—is a form of *kiai* that non-vocally expresses the individual's degree of ire, and perhaps hints of what may follow if the situation persists.
- An individual whose strength or endurance is taxed will utter a type of **groan** to get themselves over the final hurdle of the challenging task. It is a sound we all emit, unconsciously but instinctively, and is a form of vocal *kiai* we use to rally the last vestiges of energy for completing our objective.
- And (hopefully less familiar) there is the situation when an individual feels so utterly thwarted or beaten by another—a bully, a co-worker, an employer—that he simply **wishes** that the other person would die. In those circumstances where speaking out or pummeling the other person to a pulp are *not* feasible options, the only seeming recourse is to **wish** *for their immediate demise*. Although this form of thought-focused kiai remains a theoretical type of application, almost every culture in the world shares in an understanding of this notion—*the Evil Eye*.

In my view, these three vehicles represent the most cogent manifestations of the many facets of kiaijutsu.

---

3 You have actually performed variations of them yourself

This photograph captures the full essence of *Shinrigaku*:
Haragei*, the non-vocal *Kiai,* and *Metsuke

SATSUJINJUTSU

Satsujinjutsu, or insight into man, was more than just instant character analysis for the ninja.

—Andrew Adams
Ninja, The Invisible Assassins

At the very end of the third chapter of the *Sonshi*, Sonbu provides this oft-quoted advice—

> *If you know the enemy and know yourself, you need not fear the result of a hundred battles.*

The sole objective of the ninja's art of **satsujinjutsu** is to acquire *insight into Man:* or simply, to *know your enemy.* To know the enemy means to know *everything* about him. While *satsujin* literally means "to murder," or "to assassinate." the less common *satsujinjutsu* refers to an ability to recognize or detect another person's capacity or proclivity toward killing, ie, *who was dangerous and who was not*.

Satsujinjutsu was not so much a specific art as it was a concept. In order to gain insight into his enemy, the *shinobi* relied on a number of interrelated disciplines. Among them were *satsujin, ninsōgaku, gojyo-goyoku*, and others that bordered on the fantastic.

The ninja had to be very skilled at assessing people. He carefully noted their mannerisms, attire, language, and gait. Moreover, he could infer economic conditions by the appearance of a house or by the fragrance a kimono gave off, as well as from the looks, attitudes, and gestures of those he observed. He began with the obvious—their *body type.*

The enemy's physical balance can reflect his mental equilibrium

Opponent Body Type

Individuals are born with an inherited body type which is determined by skeletal frame and body composition. Based on these and other factors, the ninja recognized that the variety of human body types correlated with certain temperaments and, often, fighting styles. He understood that, generally speaking—

- A relatively *big* or *heavy* opponent was likely to move slower, but his blows would be comparatively strong due to his body mass.
- A *well-toned* or *physically fit* opponent was likely to have the least physical limitations, while his blows would be comparatively fast and formidable.
- A relatively *thin* or *slight* opponent was likely to move very fast, but his blows would be comparatively weak due to lack of mass.

This crude rule-of-thumb that the ninja once used to assess an opponent has since become the established, though controversial, anthropological area known as ***somatotypes***. Having lost popularity in the mid-20th century for "political" reasons, this field is again being researched and studied, albeit with due respect for social and cultural sensitivities. The relatively big or heavy opponent is called an *endomorph*; the well-toned or physically fit opponent is a *mesomorph;* and the thin or slight opponent is an *ectomorph.*

Body Type and Temperament

Recognizing a person's body type is far easier than assessing his psychological traits because the body is, obviously, more visible than the mind; but psychological assessment is a skill that *can* be acquired through practice. The study of temperament explores how people eat, sleep, speak, walk, and fight. Temperament is body type in action.

The Endomorphic Opponent

The endomorph shows a splendid ability to eat, digest, and socialize. A good deal of his energy is oriented around food, and he enjoys sitting around after a good meal and letting the digestive process proceed without disturbance. Endomorphs live far from the upsets and nervous stomachs of the *ectomorphs*. They fall readily to sleep and their sleep is deep and easy; they lie limp and sprawled out and frequently snore. In combat, endomorphs are relaxed and slow-moving. Their breathing comes from the abdomen and is deep and regular. Their reactions are slow, and this is a reflection on a temperament level of a basal metabolism, pulse, breathing rate, and temperature which are all often slower and lower than average. It is as if all the energy is focused on the abdominal area, leaving less of it available to be expressed in the limbs and face, and giving the impression of a lack of intensity.

The Mesomorphic Opponent

The mesomorph is centered on assertiveness and a love of action. He tends to eat his food rapidly and somewhat randomly, often neglecting set meal times. He sleeps the least of the three types and sometimes contents himself with six hours. He shows an insensitivity to pain and a tendency to high blood pressure and large blood vessels. The mesomorph has no hesitation in approaching people and making known his wants and desires. The tendency to think with his muscles and find exhilaration in their use leads him to enjoy taking chances and risks, even when the actual gain is well-known to be minimal. They can become fond of gambling and are generally physically fearless. They can be either difficult and argumentative, or slow to anger, but always with the capacity to act out physically.

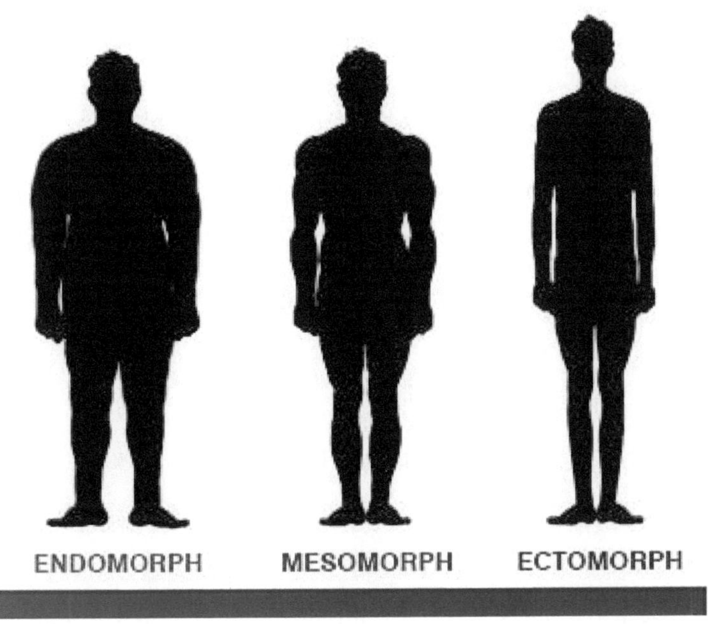

In combat, mesomorphs revert to their most fundamental form of behavior and seek action of some sort. This physical drive manifests itself on the psychological level in a sense of competition. He is unhesitating about the all-out pursuit of the goal he seeks. Associated with this trait is a certain psychological callousness. On the positive side this is called being practical and free from sentimentality, but on the negative side it is called ruthlessness or obnoxious aggression.

The Ectomorphic Opponent

The ectotomorph focuses on privacy, restraint, and a highly developed self-awareness. The outstanding characteristic of the ectomorph is his finely-tuned sensitivity to his surroundings. Since his whole organism is sensitive to stimulation, the ectomorph develops a series of characteristic strategies to cut down on stimuli.

He is like a sonar operator who must constantly be wary of a sudden loud noise breaking in on the delicate sounds he is trying to trace. He tries to avoid making noise or being subjected to it. He is a quiet sleeper, but a light one, and he is often plagued by insomnia. He tends to sleep on one side and his sleep, though slow in coming, can be hard to shake off.

In combat, the ectomorph's energy level is low, though his reactions are fast. Self-awareness is a principle trait of ectomorphs. When they are in a situation of dealing with an opponent, they often make a poor first impression. They are hypersensitive to pain because they anticipate it and have a lower pain threshold as well. This hypersensitivity leads not only to quick physical reactions but to excessively fast social reactions as well. They do not project their voices like the mesomorphs, but focus it to reach only the person they are addressing. They appear younger than their age and often wear an alert, intent expression.

There are many other metrics that contribute to ninjutsu's disciplines of *satsujinjutsu*; those, however, will require a separate book to cover.

NINSŌGAKU

Since [the ninja] was familiar with the science of physiognomy, he was able to read the facial features of his fellow man.

—Andrew Adams
Ninja, The Invisible Assassins

NINSŌGAKU, simply put, is the ability to "read" the information that time and experience have recorded on a person's face. Today, literature on the art of *ninsōgaku* is as scarce as information on the *art of ninjutsu* was fifty years ago. This scarcity exists not only in the field of martial arts in general, but also within the specific realms of traditional *bujutsu* and *ninjutsu*, those same sectors of Japan's warrior culture that once numbered *ninsōgaku* among its many requisite disciplines. One has to wonder why the heads of the various ninjutsu organizations fail to include this vital skill in their teachings today.

A quick search on the Internet, (that much-visited venue of those averse to actual academic research), reveals little or nothing on the subject of *ninsōgaku*. Although *ninsōgaku* is not exactly "physiognomy," those who use this term to search may have better results, but just minimally. This is because what is meant by *physiognomy* is not the equivalent of what the Japanese mean by *ninsōgaku*, and because physiognomy also is classified as *pseudoscience* by the politically correct. "*Pseudoscience*," we are told, "*consists of statements, beliefs, or practices that are claimed to be scientific and factual in the absence of evidence gathered and constrained by appropriate scientific methods*."

The omniscient oracle, Wikipedia, has this to say about *Physiognomy*:

> *... Credence of such study has varied from time to time. The practice was well accepted by the ancient Greek philosophers, but fell into disrepute in the Middle Ages when practiced by vagabonds and mountebanks ...*
>
> *Physiognomy, as understood in the past, meets the contemporary definition of a pseudoscience. No clear evidence indicates physiognomy works, though recent studies have suggested that facial appearances do "contain a kernel of truth" about a person's personality.*

Interestingly, similar if not identical opinions were popularly held by educated individuals in the 19th and early 20th centuries with regard to Eastern "claims" that a 98-lb woman could effectively fight off a 200-lb attacker, or that sticking thin needles in a patient's ear could allow a doctor to operate on him without anaesthesia. Is *ninsō*, then, the next incredible form of "Oriental quackery," waiting to be *suitably* explained before ultimately being accepted by the over-educated but ignorant masses?

The "evidence" that today's learned and politically-correct masses present against physiognomy existed in Japan as well, for there, too, *ninsō* was "practiced by vagabonds and mountebanks." But it was also *effectively* practiced by doctors and healers, as well as by *samurai* and *ninja* who had their lives, or the lives of others, at stake. In the end, a ninjutsu practitioner should never believe without proof—nor should he disbelieve without first testing.

Face Reading in Ancient Times

Asian methods of *face reading* have been practiced for thousands of years and the earliest records of their use date from 2697 – 2598 BC. The first written work related to face reading in Chinese Medicine is thought to be the Yellow Emperor's **Classic of Internal Medicine**, which is dated to approximately 2600 BC. This text confirms that medical practitioners had by that time already developed an in-depth knowledge of C*hi* energy, Yi*n* and Y*ang* theory, and the interrelation of the *Five Elements*. In addition, various forms of assessment were employed for observing the outside of the patient's body in order to diagnose what was happening *within* it.

By 220 BC, the Chinese had established a formalized *art of face reading*, which they call *mian xiang*, as a diagnostic tool to help assess a patient's condition. It was found especially useful in instances where the ill person was, as a symptom of his illness, unable to speak or describe his ailment. Many components of *mian xiang* were derived from Taoist philosophy, and the oldest writing on this topic is credited to an individual named *Guiguzi* 鬼谷子 (481-221 BC).

Face Reading in Japan

Close observation of the face afforded early Chinese doctors a deep knowledge of the personalities of their patients. These healers were reputed to be well-educated men with great compassion for human frailty. Apart from these doctors there were also *professional face-readers* during this time who combined the roles of priest, astrologer, and counselor. In time, the art of *mian xiang* became an established practice throughout China, eventually spreading to the neighboring countries of Japan, Korea, and India.

In Japan, face reading was initially practiced in the same manner as it had been brought from China—as a component of traditional medicine—used solely for diagnosing the ill. In time, as typically happens in Japan with all borrowed cultural influences, the art of face reading became "Japanized," to use Donn Draeger's term. The study of *Chi* energy became ***Ki***, *Yin* and *Yang* theory became ***In-Yo Ho***, the theory of the *Five Elements* became ***Gogyo Setsu*** and, as we shall see presently, *mian xiang* became *ninsōgaku*.

What Ninsōgaku is Not

In undertaking any new endeavor, it is not unusual for a novice to have preconceptions or expectations regarding what the endeavor will include or involve. Some of these will be correct; other not. Thus, before delving into what the art of ninsōgaku is, it will be helpful from the outset to clarify what it is *not*.

Ninsōgaku is not Body Language

Although the focus of ninsōgaku centers principally on the subject's countenance and, to a lesser extent on their entire body, it does *not* rely on their gestures or bodily movements. And, while the subject's face can be read in the moment, as is typically done in body language, ninsōgaku is more generally used to read the *past history* that is "engraved" on the subject's face.

Who is the *most* dangerous? You can guess—or you can *know*!

Ninsōgaku is not Mind-Reading

While in the past ninsōgaku practitioners, called *ninsōmi*, were sometimes believed to possess mind-reading capabilities, this was merely the subject's misunderstanding of the method being used. In the days when people believed that ninja tread on water, walked through solid walls, or vanished at will, it is not surprising they would mistake the learned skill of ninsōgaku for a supernatural ability

Ninsōgaku is not Cold Reading

Although a skilled *cold reader* can accurately cull and interpret data from a subject, he does so by reading gestures, demeanor, breathing, voice. culture, tone and inflection. The cold reader does *not* read the historical information recorded on the subject's face. It is for this reason that a ninsōme can read a subject by means of a photograph, but a cold reader cannot.

Ninsōgaku is not a Hobby

Ninsōgaku was not only used on a professional level in ancient Japan but also in the modern-day, as in many cases medical practitioners still utilize the art as a component of their diagnostic processes.

Ninsōgaku—the lines on the face "write a record" of that person's health and history

Ninsōgaku as a *Bushi* and *Shinobi* Practice

Owing to the efficacy of face reading in determining a person's condition, it was inevitable that Japan's warrior culture—which already used this knowledge on the battlefield to assess the hurt or wounded—soon found an *alternate use* for face reading. Thus it was that *martial* applications for face reading eventually developed to serve the *bushi* and *shinobi.*

In this context, it must be noted, face reading was part of a larger discipline called *satsujinjutsu*, already introduced in the previous chapter. Such disciplines of face reading and opponent assessment allowed warriors to better heed Sonbu's dictum to, *Know Your Enemy.*

Insight into Your Opponent

Both the *bushi* and *shinobi* understood that a person's face carries written on it his/her personality traits, combat predilections, physical skills, and even depth of training. The importance of knowing to read a potential opponent's face is referenced in both **The Fighting Spirit of Japan** (Harrison) and **Ninja, The Invisible Assassins** (Adams) as a required skill of feudal age warriors.

Ninsōgaku provided the *bushi* and *shinobi* skilled in its methods with valuable information they could use for strategy and/or imminent engagement. Both types of warriors found it helpful, if not necessary, to quickly assess a potential opponent by interpreting what might be discernible on their countenance, and thus determining the best way to engage with them.

Know Your Enemy, Know Your Friend

At its most basic level, the skillful practice of ninsōgaku, affords three fundamental assessments by which we can know a subject, regardless of whether the person is clearly identified as an adversary or merely demonstrate proclivities for becoming one. The first assessment that ninsōgaku allows us to make is simply the determination of whether the subject is a friend, a foe, or someone undecided.

The *second* assessment it allows is estimating the *degree* of their amity, enmity, or uncertainty. The *third* assessment ninsōgaku can provide is an indication of how that friendship, antagonism, or indecision will manifest toward us in extreme circumstances.

Allies and Adversaries

In ninjutsu, the ability to read another person's face is not solely relevant for recognizing a potential enemy, but also to better assess and understand one's allies. Those who we may rely or depend on are subject to personal life challenges that we are not always aware of; challenges that nonetheless may affect their abilities or roles as allies. A challenged ally can be offered assistance or support; a compromised ally must be guarded against or appropriately marginalized. In either case, it is as necessary to study our presumed friends as it is to measure our known or potential enemies. By doing so we can remain vigilant in the event that the former become the latter.

GOJYO-GOYOKU

The Five Character Flaws

In the world of stealth and espionage, the ability to skillfully influence the people around us as "human assets" is critical to the positive outcomes of commissioned or personal objectives. To accomplish this in Sengoku time, the historical *shinobi* used *Gojyo Goyoku-no-Kotowari—the Principle of the Five Character Flaws*—to influence or manipulate a person. If that sounds distasteful to you, I agree with you; but then perhaps you should go back to training in *ninpo* and leave the practice of ninjutsu to the adults.

Gojyo *The Five Character Flaws*

The historical *shinobi* understood that the people he relied on—call them targets, subjects, or assets—might at times be temperamental, variable, or unpredictable to manage, even if he was skilled at *satsujinjutsu* (character assessment) and *ninsōgaku* (face reading). Therefore the ability to skillfully influence the people he interacted with was critical to the positive outcomes of the ninja's objectives. To accomplish this, the historical *shinobi* kept one additional skill in his arsenal of psychological weapons and tools: *Gojyo-goyoku!*

The ninja's use of *gojyo-goyoku* derived from an understanding of Buddhist principles, specifically the five *weaknesses* or *flaws* that Buddhism are advises its followers to avoid or to moderate. The ninja knew that each individual exhibits one major character flaw, one that he could discover and exploit. The five *weaknesses* or *flaws* to avoid in excess are:

- **Kyosha** (timidity, cowardice, or fear);
- **Rakusha** (laziness and lack of initiative);
- **Dosha** (anger and rashness);
- **Kisha** (pleasure and self-indulgence); and
- **Aisha** (sympathy and soft-heartedness).

The historical *shinobi* understood that the ability to manipulate others is a valuable, if not critical, skill: not only to accomplish his ends but also to prevent being manipulated himself. That was in the 15th century; however, times change but people don't. That is why in our Ninpokai dojo, one of only a handful that provide traditional shinrigaku instruction, gojyo-goyoku is still taught along with another three-dozen historical and traditional *shinobi* disciplines.

Perspective

Sadly, we live in a world where people are constantly seeking to get what they want from you. Your best defense is to become skilled at effectively managing them instead! But you already know that, otherwise you would only be training in punching, kicking, and throwing, instead of the many psychological ninjutsu arts that you practice!

Even the most stoic of individual around you has some sort of weak link that you can exploit to gain control over them. It is important to always pay attention to what they say and do when they are around you. By simply paying attention to others, you will not only become skilled in the fundamentals on how to *influence* them, but you'll also find the skills are applicable to business situations beyond the sphere of ninjutsu tradecraft.

Three Subconscious Needs

There are three main goals that all targets subconsciously seek:

1) *Symbolic rewards*
2) *Material rewards* and
3) *Security*

Symbolic rewards

We all have the need for symbolic rewards, such as recognition and praise. Everybody wants to feel important and special. The act of praising and recognizing another is a strong motivator. Always reward good deeds with praise, and give positive, constructive criticism for bad deeds. If you are patient, in time you will see the results of your compliments.

Material rewards

Material rewards mean a lot to targets, whether they realize it or not. In any capitalist society, a person's status is judged by his material gains. Therefore, since money produces material gain, it is a strong motivator, and its presence can have a strong influence on others.

Security

Everyone needs security and stability. Security is attained when targets feel they belong and are needed by others. Targets want security in their jobs, friends, family, etc. There are many ways to increase targets' feelings of security:

- Let targets know what you have to offer and what you expect from them in return. Explain why the relationship you have with them is the way it is.
- Make targets feel that they are needed and belong in the relationship with you. Show a need for their presence.
- Let targets know what their efforts are accomplishing and how they are affecting you. Make them feel important and special to you. Show them that their efforts are appreciated.
- Make sure that parties in the relationship are compatible

A Modern Shinobi Code

The English language word FLAGS serves as a useful acronym for remembering the *Five Fatal Flaws*—

Fearful	**Kyosha** (timidity, cowardice, or fear);
Lazy	**Rakusha** (laziness and lack of initiative);
Angry	**Dosha** (anger and rashness);
Greedy	**Kisha** (pleasure and self-indulgence); and
Soft-hearted	**Aisha** (sympathy and soft-heartedness).

Goyoku *The Five Desires*

A *satsujinjutsu* skill related to the Gojyo is the complementary method called *Goyoku*. Goyoku is accomplished in a similar manner as Gojyo, except that instead of five weaknesses it focuses on five excess *desires*. The five *desires* to avoid in excess are:

- **Food**—Exert influence through their desire for rich foods.
- **Sex**—Exert influence through their desire for the opposite sex.
- **Fame**—Exert influence through their desire for promotion or becoming famous
- **Property**—Exert influence through their desire for money.
- **Elegance**—Exert influence by appealing to a hobby or telling an interesting story.

Goyoku skills will not be covered here but will be included in our next *Shinobi-no-Michi* volume.

SHINSHIN SHINGAN

The Eyes and Mind of God

SHINSHIN SHINGAN is a *shinobi* expression that reminds us to enter all situations, whether new or familiar, with "*the mind and the eyes of God.*" It has been inadequately compared to the overused term "situational awareness," but magnified a hundredfold. As such, it is perhaps one of the most vital principles to espouse at this time.

Although precious little has been left to us on this subject in the many historical ninja manuals that have survived till today, there are relevant words of advice written by Allen W. Dulles, who served as Chief of Station for the OSS during WWII, and later became the sixth, and longest-serving, director of the CIA.

Among his *Seventy-Three Rules for Spies* he devised for intelligence operatives, Dulles wrote:

- The greatest vice in the game is that of carelessness. Mistakes made generally cannot be rectified.

- Security consists not only in avoiding big risks. It consists in carrying out daily tasks with painstaking remembrance of the tiny things that security demands. The little things are in many ways more important than the big ones. It is they which oftenest give the game away. It is consistent care in them, which form the habit and characteristic of security mindedness.

- In any case, the man or woman who does not indulge in the daily security routine, boring and useless though it may sometimes appear, will be found lacking in the proper instinctive reaction when dealing with the bigger issues.
- There are many virtues to be striven after in the job. The greatest of them all is security. All else must be subordinated to that.

However it is accomplished, the ultimate goal of security-mindedness is keeping you safe. It is the same goal you strive for when attempting to develop the *Mind and the Eyes of God*. Securitymindedness generates a sense of *shinshin shingan*.

Shinshin Shingan—the Mind and Eyes of God

While it once served the ninja to foresee an attack waiting behind a door or a trap at a meeting with a treacherous friend, today *shinshin shingan* must function to keep you healthy and safe from exposure. As Dulles would have agreed, carelessness and a lax attitude are the doors by which a threat enters.

心理学

End Word

Many ninjutsu practitioners you meet today will casually assert, by word or by attitude, that they are among the rare breed who practice *the True and Ancient Art of the Ninja*. Too often, you have to bite your tongue "till it bleeds" to keep from laughing at their claims.

You walk way from these friendly conversations, congratulating yourself for your patience and endurance in the presence of such illiterates. You try to recall how many times you had to stifle a chuckle: there was the *colorful uniform*, then the *made-up title*, the bought or *self-awarded rank*, and the extensive *mastery of the Japanese language* —evidenced by how many times they said *osu* ...

After the laughter you wonder, *How can such people purport to "walk the path," when they don't even know the history of the art they claim to have mastered or the mental strategies that historically took precedence over the physical skills of common combat*?

But then you gather your thoughts, regain your composure, cease thinking about your conversational partner's claims of deadly skills and lethal abilities—and you realize something that they never will: that their *boasting*, *overconfidence*, and *lack of humility* are what would enable you to sense their approach and thoroughly *negate* them —without their ever realizing what just happened ...

***Taijutsu** is great—but **Ninjutsu** will beat it every time.*

A MIND DISCIPLINES GLOSSARY

***Art of War*, The**	English language name given to the Chinese military treatise called the *Bing Fa*, below
Banpen Fugyo	Literally, "Ten thousand changes, no surprise."
Bing Fa	Chinese name of a military treatise, dating to the Fifth Century BC
Bushi	Literally, "military person or warrior"; a samurai
Bugei	Literally, "military craft;" those traditional Japanese fighting arts developed and practiced prior to 1868.
Enzan-no-Metsuke	Literally, "Gazing at the far mountain."
Fudoshin	Literally, "immovable mind."
Haragei	Literally, "Stomach art or craft."
Kanja	Japanese term for a *spy*. May or may not refer to a *shinobi*
Kunoichi	Modern fabricated term intended to denote *a woman practiced in the art of Ninjutsu*, correctly known as *shinobi-no-onna.*
Ninja	Modern term denoting a *specialist in Ninjutsu*, the Japanese Art of Espionage. See also, *Shinobi*
Ninjutsu	Modern term for the Japanese *Art of Espionage.* See also, *Shinobijutsu*
Ninsogaku	Literally, "The study of the face."
Ninsomi	A practitioner skilled in ninsogaku; a face-reader

Samurai	Literally, "one who serves." An alternate name for *bushi*, or warrior. Contrary to common belief, a samurai could serve as a ninja, and a ninja could be a samurai or come from samurai lineage
Sengoku Jidai	Japan's *Warring States Era* (1467 – 1603); alternately called the *Age of Civil Wars*
Shinobi , Shinobu	Japanese term for a *specialist in espionage* or any number of the covert activities of *Shinobijutsu;* the original term for *ninja*
Shinobijutsu	Japanese *Art of Espionage and Subterfuge*
Shinobi-no-Michi	The *Path of Patience, of Secrecy*, and *of Stealth.* It is a difficult path to walk, for it must be traversed in anonymity and humility.
Shinrigaku	Literally, *the Study of the Mind; psychology. A term sometimes used to describe the warrior's knowledge of enemy behavior*
Shinshin Shingan	Literally, *God mind-God eyes. The developed ability to know or sense everything going on around you*
Sonbu	Japanese transliteration for *Sun Wu Tzu*, another name for Sun Tzu (the presumed author of *The Art of War*)
Sonshi	Japanese name for *The Art of War*
Sun Tzu	One of various Chinese names (alternately, *Sun Wu Tzu*, *Sun Wu*, *Sunzi*) ascribed to a warrior-sage thought to have written the *Bing Fa*
Taijutsu	Literally, "body skills or arts." Pre-jujutsu era Japanese term for a number of *fighting arts*; an early term for *jujutsu*, and generally conflated with the Art of Ninjutsu

APPENDICES

Appendix A:

SUN TZU AND THE USE OF SPIES

Sonbu said:

Raising a host of a hundred thousand men and marching them great distances entails heavy loss on the people and a drain on the resources of the State. The daily expenditure will amount to a thousand ounces of silver. There will be commotion at home and abroad, and men will drop down exhausted on the highways. As many as seven hundred thousand families will be impeded in their labor.

Hostile armies may face each other for years, striving for the victory which is decided in a single day. This being so, to remain in ignorance of the enemy's condition simply because one grudges the outlay of a hundred ounces of silver in honors and emoluments, is the height of inhumanity.

One who acts thus is no leader of men, no present help to his sovereign, no master of victory.

Thus, what enables the wise sovereign and the good general to strike and conquer, and achieve things beyond the reach of ordinary men, is foreknowledge.

Now this foreknowledge cannot be elicited from spirits; it cannot be obtained inductively from experience, nor by any deductive calculation.

Knowledge of the enemy's dispositions can only be obtained from other men.

Hence the use of spies, of whom there are five classes.

Local spies
Internal spies
Turned spies
Expendable spies
Surviving spies

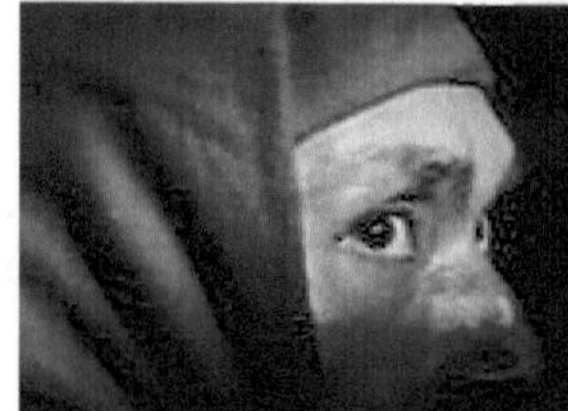

Knowledge of the enemy's dispositions can only be obtained from other men. Hence the use of spies...

When these five kinds of spy are all at work, none can discover the secret system. This is called ***The Divine Manipulation of the Threads***. It is the sovereign's most precious faculty.

Having *local* spies means employing the services of the inhabitants of a district.

Having *internal* spies, making use of officials of the enemy.

Having *turned* spies, getting hold of the enemy's spies and using them for our own purposes.

Having *expendable* spies, doing certain things openly for purposes of deception, and allowing our spies to know of them and report them to the enemy.

Surviving spies, finally, are those who bring back news from the enemy's camp.

Hence it is that which none in the whole army are more intimate relations to be maintained than with spies. None should be more liberally rewarded. In no other business should greater secrecy be preserved.

Spies cannot be usefully employed without a certain intuitive sagacity.

They cannot be properly managed without benevolence and straight-forwardness.

Without subtle ingenuity of mind, one cannot make certain of the truth of their reports.

Be subtle! be subtle! and use your spies for every kind of business.

If a secret piece of news is divulged by a spy before the time is ripe, he must be put to death together with the man to whom the secret was told.

Whether the object be to *crush an army*, to *storm a city*, or to *assassinate an individual*, it is always necessary to begin by finding out the names of the attendants, the aides-de-camp, and door-keepers and sentries of the general in command. Our spies must be commissioned to ascertain these.

The enemy's spies who have come to spy on us must be sought out, tempted with bribes, led away and comfortably housed. Thus they will become turned spies and available for our service.

It is through the information brought by the turned spy that we are able to acquire and employ local and internal spies.

It is owing to his information, again, that we can cause the expendable spy to carry false tidings to the enemy.

Lastly, it is by his information that the surviving spy can be used on appointed occasions.

The end and aim of spying in all its five varieties is *knowledge of the enemy*; and this knowledge can only be derived, in the first instance, from the turned spy. Hence it is essential that the turned spy be treated with the utmost liberality.

Of old, the rise of the Yin dynasty was due to *I Chih* who had served under the Hsia. Likewise, the rise of the Chou dynasty was due to *Lu Ya* who had served under the Yin.

Hence it is only the enlightened ruler and the wise general who will use the highest intelligence of the army for purposes of spying and thereby they achieve great results. Spies are a most important element in water, because on them depends an army's ability to move.

Appendix B:

SENGOKU JIDAI—THE AGE OF CIVIL WARS

The **Sengoku Jidai**, or Age of Civil Wars, was a turbulent time in Japanese history (c. 1467 – c. 1603) marked by social upheaval, political intrigue, and near-constant military conflict. It lasted from 1467 to 1603, coming to an end when all political power was unified under Tokugawa Ieyasu.

Although the Emperor of Japan was officially the ruler of his nation and every lord swore loyalty to him, he was largely a marginalized, ceremonial, and religious figure during this period, and delegated his power to the *Shogun*. In time, many of the daimyo began to fight each other for control over land and influence over the Shogunate.

Monsho (Crests) **of Different Daimyo**

At the beginning of the 15th century, the suffering caused by earthquakes and famines often served to trigger armed uprisings by farmers weary of debt and taxes. The Ōnin War, a conflict rooted in economic distress and brought on by a dispute over Shogunal succession, is generally regarded as the onset of the Sengoku period. Fighting in and around Kyoto lasted for nearly eleven years, leaving the city almost completely destroyed. The conflict in Kyoto then spread to outlying provinces.

The upheaval resulted in the further weakening of central authority, and throughout Japan regional lords, called ***daimyo***, rose to fill the vacuum. In the course of this power shift, well-established clans such as the **Takeda** and the **Imagawa**, who had ruled under the authority of both the Kamakura and Muromachi bakufu, were able to expand their spheres of influence.

Japan during the Warring States Era

Unification

After nearly a century of political instability and warfare, Japan was on the verge of unification by **Oda Nobunaga**, who had risen from obscurity to dominate central Japan. When Oda was assassinated by one of his generals, Akechi Mitsuhide, in 1582, it provided Toyotomi Hideyoshi—one of Oda's most trusted generals—the opportunity to establish himself as Oda's successor. Though he was ineligible for the title of shogun due to his common birth, Toyotomi eventually consolidated his control over the remaining daimyōs.

Fourth Battle of Kawanakashima

When Toyotomi died in 1598 without a successor, the country was once again thrust into political turmoil. On his deathbed, Toyotomi appointed a group of the most powerful lords in Japan—*Tokugawa Ieyasu, Maeda Toshiie, Ukita Hideie, Uesugi Kagekatsu,* and *Mōri Terumoto*—intending for them to govern as the *Council of Five Regents* until his infant son, Hideyori, came of age. An uneasy peace lasted one year until the death of Maeda and, in 1599, a number of high-ranking figures, notably Ishida Mitsunari, accused Tokugawa Ieyasu of disloyalty to the Toyotomi regime.

This led to the ***Battle of Sekigahara*** in 1600, during which Tokugawa and his allies, who controlled the east of the country, defeated the anti-Tokugawa forces, which had control of the west. Regarded as the last major conflict of the Sengoku period, Tokugawa's victory at Sekigahara effectively marked the end of the Toyotomi regime, the last remnants of which were finally destroyed in the Siege of Osaka in 1615.

Tokugawa Clan Mon

Tokugawa Ieyasu received the title *Shogun* in 1603, and abdicated in favour of his son, Tokugawa Hidetada, in 1605 (while retaining real control himself), to emphasize the family's hereditary hold on the post; he thus established Japan's final shogunate, which lasted until the Meiji Restoration in 1868.

Appendix C:

BUGEI JUHAPPAN—THE MARTIAL CURRICULUM

The terms **Koryū Bugei** and **Koryū Bujutsu** refer to *classical Japanese martial traditions* that evolved prior to Japan's Edo era, 1868. Later martial traditions, created after 1868, are categorized as **Gendai Budo**, or *modern martial ways*, even if they share similar characteristics and philosophies to the earlier warrior traditions.

The original martial traditions possess an unbroken lineage of direct transmission of the system from master to pupil. While some later traditions of the **Edo Jidai**[4] focus on perhaps a single weapon or other aspect of martial culture, the earlier systems created during the **Sengoku Jidai**, the *Warring States Era*, generally reflected a comprehensive martial curriculum comprised of unarmed combat, weaponry, strategy, and other elements of martial study.

These curricula are typically comprised of eighteen discrete warrior arts or disciplines and are thus called the **Bugei Juhappan**, or *18 Disciplines of War*. The plural term curricula is used because there was no one standard curriculum of 18 warrior disciplines. That is to say, each of the different warrior families determined which particular 18 disciplines served them best.

The untold number of martial arts that existed throughout the Sengoku era could mean that the Bugei Juhappan of one family might be quite distinct from that of the neighboring clans. Thus, there have been many different versions of the Bugei Juhappan, reflecting the differing needs of the time. Although the Bugei Juhappan vary *greatly* from family to family, the following list has been suggested as a typical example among the *bushi*:

- **Taijutsu** Unarmed combat
- **Tantojutsu** Dagger techniques
- **Kenjutsu** Sword techniques
- **Juttejutsu** Iron truncheon techniques
- **Bojutsu** Staff techniques

4 These are still regarded as *koryū* although they were developed in the relatively peaceful era of Tokugawa shogunate

- **Kusarigamajutsu** Chain and Sickle techniques
- **Soujutsu** Spear techniques
- **Naginatajutsu** Halberd techniques
- **Shurikenjutsu** Blade throwing techniques
- **Kyujutu** Archery
- **Hojutsu** Firearms techniques
- **Hojojutsu** Tying and restraining with ropes
- **Bajutsu** Horsemanship
- **Suiren** Combat swimming
- **Chikujojutsu** Fortification methods
- **Gunpo Heiho** Battlefield strategy
- **Chimon** Geography
- **Shinobijutsu** Stealth and Espionage techniques

The shinobi traditions would have their own concept of what a set of martial disciplines might encompass. Many such lists exist, and the one below is an example. Note the areas of overlap with the *bushi's* bugei juhappan, as well as those disciplines that were unique to ninjutsu.

- **Taijutsu** Unarmed combat
- **Kenjutsu** Sword techniques
- **Bojutsu** Staff techniques
- **Soujutsu** Spear techniques
- **Fukumi-bari** Blowing needles
- **Shurikenjutsu** Blade throwing techniques
- **Kayakujutsu** Arson and demolitions
- **Hojojutsu** Rope-binding and restraining techniques
- **Nawanuke-no-jutsu** Escape from restraints
- **Hensojutsu** Disguises
- **Suiren** Combat swimming
- **Boryaku** Strategy
- **Shinobi-iri** Stealth and infiltration techniques
- **Intonjutsu** Escape and evasion techniques
- **Gotonjutsu** Hiding and concealment techniques
- **Tenmon** Meteorology
- **Chimon** Geography
- **Choho** Espionage and Intelligence

About the Author

In 1984, James Loriega founded the **New York Ninpokai**, a training facility which soon came to be regarded as "*the premier academy for the traditional shinobi arts in NYC.*" Loriega began his formal martial arts training in 1967 with the late Grandmaster Ronald Duncan, the first non-Japanese to teach the shinobi arts in the United States—and the acknowledged *Father of American Ninjutsu.* Though he later trained with other ninjutsu masters, it was from Duncan-sensei that Loriega learned the myriad strategies, tactics, techniques, and disciplines of the ancient *shinobi.*

During the mid- to late-80s, Loriega also studied other Japanese martial arts, including *Aikijujutsu, Taijutsu, Jojutsu, and Hojojutsu.* Loriega began writing extensively around that same time, and from 1985 to 1995 served as Technical Consultant and Contributing Editor for **Ninja** magazine, an international publication dedicated exclusively to ninjutsu.

His overseas travels to teach ninjutsu also exposed Loriega to the western martial arts of Europe and the Mediterranean, and his subsequent training in those arts led to instructor ranks in other disciplines.

In January of 2002, Loriega was recognized as a master in western arts by the *International Masters-at-Arms Federation* (IMAF), based in Milan, Italy. The IMAF, now dissolved, was an organization of professional instructors of Historical and Classical edged weapons.

In February of 2018, he was recognized by the *Martial Arts University* as a *Martial Arts Icon*—an individual who is symbolic of an idea and leaves a memorable mark on the lives of those he teaches.

In April of 2018, he was recognized as a *Ninjutsu Scholar* and inducted into the *International Circle of Masters* (ICM).

Loriega holds instructor ranks in Ninjutsu, Jujutsu, and Aikijujutsu, as well as in a number of Western martial arts.

He has published over a dozen books on martial arts and martial culture, and his extensive writings have appeared in mainstream martial arts publications such as **Black Belt**, **Inside Kung-Fu**, **Ninja**, and **Tactical Knives**.

Inquiries for seminars or workshops may be sent to:

Ninpokai@aol.com

BIBLIOGRAPHY

Adams, Andrew. **Ninja, *The Invisible Assassins*.** Burbank, Ca: Ohara Publication. 1971

Cummins, Antony. **Iga and Koka Ninja**: *Skills The Secret Shinobi Scrolls of Chikamatsu Shigenori*. Gloucestershire, UK: The History Press. 2013

Draeger, Donn F. and Robert W. Smith. **Asian Fighting Arts**. Tokyo, New York, San Francisco: Kodansha International, Ltd. 1969

– **Ninjutsu, *The Art of Invisibility*.** Tokyo: Lotus Press. 1971

– **Classical Bujutsu**. New York: John Weatherhill, Inc. 1973

Gilbey, John. (Pseudonym for Robert W. Smith) **Secret Fighting Arts of the World**. Rutland, Vt. and Tokyo, Japan: Tuttle. 1963

Gluck, Jay, **Zen Combat**. New York: Ballantine Books. 1962

Hayes, Stephen K.**The Ninja** *and their Secret Fighting Art.* Rutland, Vt. and Tokyo, Japan: Tuttle. 1981

Loriega, James. **Ninsogaku:** *Ninjutsu's Art of Face Reading*. New York: Lost Arts Publications. 2017

– **Katsura Otoko:** *Ninjutsu for the Lone Practitioner.* New York: Lost Arts Publications. 2018

– **Ninjutsu in the Articles of Sun Tzu**. New York: Lost Arts Publications. 2018

– **The Lost Writings of Ninjutsu**. New York: Lost Arts Publications. 2019

– **Understanding Ninjutsu**. New York: Lost Arts Publications. 2019

– **Zankanjo**: *The Code of Shinobi.* New York: Lost Arts Publications. 2019

Seiko, Fujita. **What Is Ninjutsu?** Eric Shahan, translator. CreateSpace Independent Publishing. 2017

– **The Eighteen Weapons of War**. Eric Shahan, translator. CreateSpace Independent Publishing. 2017

Sun Tzu. **The Art of War.** Lionel Giles, translator. London: Lozac. 1910

Yagyu Munenori. **The Sword and the Mind**. Hiraoki Sato, translator. New York: The Overlook Press. 1986

MRES 21.02.30

www.ingramcontent.com/pod-product-compliance
Ingram Content Group UK Ltd.
Pitfield, Milton Keynes, MK11 3LW, UK
UKHW040557210726
13854UKWH00007B/1371